SUTTER'S FORT: EMPIRE ON THE SACRAMENTO

was a most welcome sight for many wet, hungry, and exhausted pioneers traveling westward in the 1840's, for Captain John A. Sutter offered food and shelter to settlers passing near his fort, as well as work to any who wanted it.

This dramatic account, graphically illustrated by period prints and photographs, brings to life again the exciting years when Sutter's Fort flourished as a nearly self-sufficient colony in California, a dream come true for Captain Sutter. The adventuresome Sutter established his vast empire on unsettled land populated primarily by Indians, who served as his workers but who often were rebellious enemies as well. The authors describe in detail how Sutter's empire began, grew, and fell to ruin during years which included the Mexican War and the great California Gold Rush. Sutter oversaw his colony with a military-like rule and entertained his visitors, among whom were Kit Carson and John Frémont, in princely fashion. This story of Sutter's Fort includes the Indian raids, wild animal hunts, encounters with wild grizzly bears, cattle roundups, and everyday life that were a part of the fort when it existed.

This book is part of the *How They Lived* series, designed to give young people a wider and more comprehensive view of American history, and thus a deeper understanding and more lasting appreciation of their heritage.

SUTTER'S FORT: Empire on the Sacramento

SUTTER'S FORT
Empire on the Sacramento

BY WILLARD AND CELIA LUCE

ILLUSTRATED BY PAUL FRAME

GARRARD PUBLISHING COMPANY
CHAMPAIGN, ILLINOIS

Picture credits:

Contents

1. John Bidwell Arrives at
   Sutter's Fort   7
2. Building the Fort 16
3. The Indians 30
4. Vaqueros 42
5. Sutter's Army 56
6. Activities at the Fort 60
7. A Young Settler Tells
   About Sutter's Fort 70
8. Gold! 81
   Glossary 93
   Index 94

1. John Bidwell Arrives at Sutter's Fort

John Bidwell first saw Sutter's Fort on a wet, dreary November day. Bidwell and his three companions were soaked, exhausted, and hungry. They stopped beneath a large oak tree while John Bidwell rubbed his hands across his eyes to clear his vision. There through the dripping mist stood a large house. It stood on a slight hill with scattered oak and sycamore trees. The house was partly surrounded by walls still under construction. In a corral outside the fort, several horses and mules stood listlessly in the mud and rain.

They faced the newcomers and raised their ears questioningly, but they were too miserable to show greater interest.

Only twenty-two years old, Bidwell was a trail-weary man, thinned down to muscle and bone. His eyes were sunken, his cheeks hollow. His soggy clothing was ripped and torn. Bidwell noticed smoke rising from beyond the fort walls. The one-time teacher grinned at his three companions and they moved on.

They passed several grass shacks that looked like small, rounded haystacks. As they passed, the grass was parted, and strange Indian faces peered out at them.

Bidwell shivered under his wet clothing and thought, "So this is California, the land of sunshine!"

The four men rode through the gateway, their horses' feet making sharp sucking sounds in the mud.

Shops and rooms had been built against the inside of the finished section of the fort wall. From a far corner came the rosy glow of a fire and the clanging of a blacksmith's hammer. Somewhere a dog barked half-heartedly.

From close at hand, a door opened. A heavy-set man stood in the doorway. He wore

John Augustus Sutter, proud owner of Sutter's Fort
and ruler of an "empire" on the Sacramento River

store clothes, and in his left hand he carried
a large, black, flat-brimmed hat. Waving the
hat, he called out to them, "Come in! Come
in and get warm!" Flickering firelight made
a warm glow at his back. This man was John
Augustus Sutter, owner of the fort.

As they stepped down from their saddles, an
Indian appeared to take their horses. The men
kicked the mud from their feet and stepped
into a small room. The few men in the room
moved back against the adobe walls as Sutter
urged the newcomers close to the small fireplace. While Bidwell and his companions held
out their hands to the fire, Sutter poured each

9

of them a cup of coffee. "Drink this," he urged. "It'll help warm you up." Sutter held himself as stiff and straight as an army officer, but his blue eyes were friendly with welcome. Little drops of rain glittered on his sandy hair and mustache.

In no time at all large wooden bowls of beef and bread were brought from the kitchen across the courtyard. The four men gulped the coffee and wolfed down the food. For three days they had had nothing to eat.

With his stomach full and his body once more warm, John Bidwell looked around the room. It was a tiny room with two wooden chairs and a small table. The fire in the corner fireplace and candles held by brackets on the wall gave the only light. The floor was dirt.

More men crowded into the room. In one corner stood a large man wearing a leather apron. This was Peter Lassen, Sutter's blacksmith. Three Mexican *vaqueros*, or horsemen, grinned politely, their white teeth glistening in the flickering light. One man, a Negro, was the cooper, or barrel maker. According to John Sutter, he was the first Negro ever to come to the valley.

NORTHERN CALIFORNIA

1. Yerba Buena, where
Sutter landed

2. New Helvetia, where
Captain Sutter built
his fort

3. Monterey, where the
Captain received his
Mexican citizenship

4. Fort Ross, which he
bought from Russia

5. Sonoma, where a few
Americans declared
California free

6. Coloma, where gold
was discovered near
Sutter's Mill

Other men were crowding into the room next door. Bidwell could see them through the small doorway. Sutter himself and all his men were interested in the travelers and in news from the United States.

This was the year of 1841, and California belonged to Mexico. Sutter's Fort, located near the junction of the Sacramento and American Rivers, was a lonely fort. There were few neighbors and few visitors. Slowly John Bidwell and his companions told of their journey.

Five months before, they had left Missouri for California with a wagon train. John Bartleson, a Missouri farmer, had been elected captain of the 69 men, women, and children. The party was well-equipped with wagons, horses, mules, and oxen. The trip had gone fairly well until over half the members left the party to go to Oregon instead. That left 31 men, one woman, and one child to find their way across the Nevada desert and over the peaks of the Sierra Nevada to California.

Real leadership soon disappeared. Wagons broke down and were left. The oxen were killed and eaten one by one. Years later John Bidwell retold the story in a book called *Echoes of the Past*. He wrote, "When we killed our last ox, we shot and ate crows or anything we could kill, and one man shot a wildcat. We could eat anything."

In this way they had finally arrived at a ranch a hundred miles or so south of Sutter's. Most went on from there to the settlements on the coast, but John Bidwell and his three companions decided to turn northward and look for John Sutter and his settlement on the Sacramento River. Here, they had been told, they would find food, shelter, and work.

It took the men eight days traveling through cold, dripping rains. Rivers and streams were overflowing. In his book John Bidwell wrote, "There were no roads, merely paths, trodden only by Indians and wild game. We were compelled to follow the paths, for the moment our animals stepped to one side, down they went into the mire."

Game was hard to shoot. Their powder soon became wet and wouldn't fire. For the last three days they had wearily plodded along without food of any kind.

They were among the first of many to be welcomed by John Sutter after struggling over the Sierra Nevada. Some travelers arrived wet, hungry, and exhausted as did John

Livestock, too, suffered on the long journey across desert and mountains to California. These oxen and mules have collapsed at Rabbit Hole Springs.

Bidwell. Others arrived in good condition. Some were brought in by rescue parties sent out by John Sutter himself. Some didn't arrive at all. Exhausted and worn out, they died along the trail.

John Sutter welcomed all that did make it. He offered them food and shelter and, if they wanted it, jobs at the fort. Bidwell described it this way: "Sutter was one of the most liberal and hospitable of men. Everybody was welcome—one man or a hundred, it was all the same." Bidwell himself was hired as one of Sutter's chief assistants. Over the years he proved himself a loyal and able worker.

2. Building the Fort

Although still not completed, Sutter's Fort was two years old at the time that John Bidwell arrived. John Sutter had reached the Sacramento Valley in August, 1839. His arrival and welcome had been very different from Bidwell's.

In 1834 at the age of 31 John Sutter had left his wife and four children in Europe and set out for America. Five years of traveling had taken him to New York; across the United States to Oregon; to the Hawaiian Islands and Alaska; and finally to California, which was then a part of Mexico. Everywhere he stopped he tried to meet important people and to get letters of introduction from them. In this way he was able to meet more important people. Sometime during this traveling he first dreamed his "dream of empire," seeing himself at the head of a vast settlement, controlling it, ruling it. Perhaps it was then that he started calling himself "Captain" Sutter.

Soon after arriving in California, Sutter traveled to Monterey, the Mexican capitol of California, to call on Juan Bautista Alvarado, the Governor. He told the Governor of his dream of establishing a colony, possibly in the Sacramento Valley. Alvarado was delighted. At that time the valley was inhabited only by Indians who were sometimes troublesome. If John Sutter could control them, it would be a great help to the California government. "Take all the land you want," the Governor had said. "Come back to Monterey in a year, and I will make you a Mexican citizen and give you a deed."

Then Sutter sailed up the Sacramento River with two rented schooners full of food, tools, weapons, and other goods necessary for the establishment of a large colony. The schooners also carried workmen.

In his head John Sutter carried the plans for his colony. A fort would be built on high land for protection, but the colony must stretch out almost endlessly over the swamps and grasslands, include the dry rolling hills, and reach far into the timber-covered mountains. There would be huge herds of the half-wild, longhorn Mexican cattle; herds of the beautiful, hardy California horses; and big flocks of sheep. He would have orchards and vineyards, acres of wheat and other grains. He would build sawmills, tanneries, and a factory for weaving blankets. He would train an army to protect it all with himself at its head.

Now John Sutter was still looking for the right spot to start his dream colony. He decided to sail ahead of the two schooners in the smaller boat manned by four of his workers. For days they pushed ahead, exploring every bay, inlet, and swamp. But nowhere could he find high land upon which to build his fort.

The small boat rounded a sudden bend in the river, and Sutter saw over a hundred Indians lining the river bank. Their faces and bodies were painted black and red and yellow. They stood motionless, holding their bows and arrows ready. They stared hard at the men in

These California Indians were painted by a Russian artist at a Spanish mission in California in 1816.

the tiny boat. John Sutter could feel the threat of their silence pushing at him, daring him to start a fight.

Sutter thought longingly of the two schooners down the river. But they were too far away to help.

Hearing sounds behind him, he glanced back to see his men raising their guns. "Put down those guns," he said quietly. "Do you want to get us killed?" His men stared at him until he repeated, "Put them down!"

Reluctantly they lowered their guns. "Now row me in. Keep the guns ready, but don't fire unless I'm attacked."

After a moment's hesitation, the men again grasped their oars. The tiny boat touched the shore, and John Sutter stepped out. He extended empty hands to show that he came unarmed. Silently he looked over the painted throng. Could any of these be Indians who had gone to school in the Spanish missions along the California coast? Could they speak the Spanish language?

Slowly Sutter raised his arms and called out, "*Amigos,*" the Spanish word for "friends."

One of the Indians stepped forward. Uneasily he asked, "Do you come in war?" He, too, spoke in Spanish.

"No," John Sutter said. "I come in peace."

The young brave dropped his bow and arrows and strode forward to meet Sutter. The others, both Indians and whites, watched carefully, not sure of the outcome.

"I have come to live among you," said Sutter as he walked toward the Indian.

Much talk followed. Sutter told the Indians of the two loaded schooners that were still down the river. "When I find the place for

my settlement and my goods arrive, I will give you presents," he promised.

The Indians nodded happily.

The next day Captain Sutter found the spot for his fort. It was on a hill two miles from the river.

"I'll call my colony New Helvetia, in honor of my home country," he said. *Helvetia* is the Latin word for Switzerland.

The schooners, the *Isabella* and the *Nicholas*, arrived and were unloaded. The crew stacked the goods in a large pile on the river bank. There they pitched tents, mounted three cannons, and placed smaller guns and ammunition close at hand.

After all this had been done, Sutter gave trinkets to the Indians who flocked into camp. They seemed friendly enough now, but John Sutter took no chances. Fires lighted the area all night long. Guards moved ceaselessly back and forth, peering into the darkness. Every hour Sutter came out of his tent. He moved watchfully through the camp, followed by his huge bulldog.

The night passed peacefully, and the next morning the schooners prepared to go back to San Francisco.

As the schooners moved out into the river, Sutter fired his cannons in salute. According to the captain of one of the schooners, their roaring vibrations ". . . produced a very remarkable effect." He wrote:

"As the heavy report of the guns and the echoes died away, the camp of the little party was surrounded by hundreds of Indians, who were excited and astonished at the unusual sound. A large number of deer, elk, and other animals on the plains were startled . . . while from the interior of the adjacent wood the howls of wolves and coyotes filled the air, and immense flocks of water fowl flew wildly about the camp."

Only a few men remained with Sutter. Three were Swiss and German. One was an Indian boy. Eight men and two women were Kanakas, natives of the Hawaiian Islands, who had come to California with him. Their first big job was to move their freight to the fort site.

This was the beginning of Sutter's Fort, New Helvetia, which later became Sacramento, the capital of the state of California.

The tiny colony needed food. One of the men walked a few hundred yards into the woods and shot an elk. The animal was immediately cleaned. The skin was stretched to dry, and all extra fat was carefully saved. Hides and tallow made from animal fat were the money of early California. Captain Sutter could use these to pay his debts, to buy goods and cattle, and to pay workmen.

The tiny colony needed shelter. One of the men, who was a carpenter, built frameworks of wood. The Kanakas cut grass and covered the frameworks, making grass huts like those of their native islands. These were comfortable but not sturdy enough for permanent homes.

Sutter's first permanent building took far more work.

First Sutter visited the Indian chiefs who lived close by. Carefully he explained that he needed workers. He would teach them what to do and how to do it. He would furnish them with food. And he would give them clothing in return for their help. Each crew was to work for two weeks, and then would be replaced by a new crew.

Before long Sutter had his first workers.

Indian workers at the fort soon learned to use crude
two-wheeled carts to haul heavy loads.

Many of the Indians living in the valley had
helped to make adobe bricks for the Spanish
missions. They were put to work digging in
the wet clay. Captain Sutter had no straw,
so part of his crew cut the tall grass that
grew nearby. This grass was mixed into the
mud to make the bricks hold together.

A carpenter made wooden molds. These were
rectangles of wood with no top or bottom.
They were placed on the ground and filled
with the mud. The top was smoothed off, the
molds removed, and the bricks left to dry in
the sun. Every day or so they were turned
over so they would dry evenly.

As these bricks dried they were laid up to make the walls of a house that was 40 feet long. Fresh mud was used to hold them together.

While the adobe bricks were being made, other Indians learned how to use the whipsaw. These long saws were used to cut boards. A log was placed on a high frame. One man stood on top of the log and another man stood below it. Each man held one end of the saw. Hour after hour they pulled the saw up and down, up and down. Slowly it cut the length of the log, ripping off rough, thick boards. These were used for floors, for window frames, and furniture.

Larger timbers to hold up the floor were squared with a broadaxe. This was much like a regular ax except that the blade might have a cutting edge of ten or twelve inches. The Indian workmen learned to use an adz to smooth the timbers. This tool resembled a thick hoe with a sharp blade.

When the house was finished it contained a blacksmith shop, a kitchen, and a private room for Sutter himself. It was completed, and the roof covered with rushes from the nearby swamps just before the autumn rains started.

The adobe brick houses and colorfully dressed people
of Monterey showed the town's Spanish origin.

One year after settling in the Sacramento
Valley, Captain Sutter traveled on horseback
from New Helvetia to Monterey. Here he
again met Governor Alvarado and received
his Mexican citizenship.

At the same time Sutter was appointed the
official representative of the local government
in the Sacramento River region. To John
Sutter this was an important honor. As he
later said, "From that time on I had the power
of life and death both over Indians and whites
in my district."

Once Sutter had his Mexican citizenship, his
appointment as official representative, and a

deed to his New Helvetia grant, he knew it was time to push ahead with his dream. The land grant of 70 square miles would require a great deal of work to develop. But first Sutter was interested in the construction of a full sized fort.

Sutter's first house had burned down during the winter. He replaced it with a larger house and surrounded a large area with walls eighteen feet high. The walls were made of adobe brick. Within the walls Sutter built a blacksmith shop and other workshops, a bakery, a blanket factory, and barracks for his soldiers. It took four years to complete.

When Sutter's Fort was completed, it boasted adobe walls, towers for defense, and busy workshops.

3. The Indians

The people of Sutter's Fort were mostly white men and Indians. Few white women and children lived there. Those who did were mostly settlers who came with their husbands and fathers and then moved on again.

Of the Indians, Sutter said, "The Indians were sometimes troublesome, but on the whole I got along very nicely with them." Sutter accomplished this by two means. First, he always paid the Indians for their work. Secondly, he punished them swiftly and severely for any disobedience of the rules he made.

One evening Sutter sat in his quarters with

an assistant. From outside they heard a sudden growl followed by a piercing scream. The two men whirled and raced for the door. Jerking it open, they stared into the pain-twisted face of an Indian. Sutter's bulldog was crouched nearby. The two men could see that the dog had attacked the Indian and had bitten his arm. They could also see that the dog was ready to spring at the Indian again.

Sutter frowned. His own blue eyes flashed sharply as he helped the Indian inside. He was thinking that his bulldog was a good watchdog and made few mistakes.

As Sutter started to question the Indian, a second scream ripped the night. Again the two men streaked for the door. They found another frightened Indian, who had been attacked and bitten by the bulldog.

By now the fort was alive with action. Questioning cries came from all directions. Men rushed through the dark, carrying burning pine knots that pushed feebly against the blackness of the night.

Some of Sutter's men caught up their rifles. Others lighted fires of driftwood that flared high. All Indians were ordered away from the buildings.

Sutter and his assistant washed and sewed up the Indians' bleeding arms. Then John Sutter asked, "Why?" He continued staring at one Indian and then the other. "I think you came to kill me," said Sutter. "Haven't I treated you fairly?"

At first they refused to look at him or to answer. Then one said, "We wanted your guns."

The other said, "We wanted your cloth."

"Your beads."

"Your—your everything." The Indian flung his uninjured arm in a half circle.

Silently Sutter thought about his need for the Indians. He needed them to make the adobe bricks and to build the wall that would enclose his fort. He needed them as vaqueros, or cowboys, to tend his cattle and sheep. He needed them to plow and to harvest. He needed them to kill the animals and stretch the hides and render the tallow.

Without Indians to do the work there could be no New Helvetia. Of this Sutter had no doubt. He also knew that if all the Indians along the Sacramento River attacked at once, there would be no New Helvetia.

At last he said to the Indians, "But you didn't get the guns."

They shook their heads.

"And you didn't get the cloth."

"No."

"Instead you got that." He pointed to their injured arms. Then he forgave them, but warned them that further attempts would be met with severe punishment. He pointed to the door and watched the Indians slip through it. Their eyes flickered fearfully in search of the bulldog.

But this threat did not stop the Indians from being "troublesome" as Sutter had hoped.

Indians around the fort acted rebelliously. They were caught with weapons hidden under their blankets. Their work slowed up. Then horses and cattle disappeared.

Finally, one day all of Sutter's workers disappeared. He found they had slipped away to a hideout 20 miles to the southeast.

There would have to be a showdown, Sutter decided. More than 10,000 Indians lived in the area. If they attacked first, Sutter, his 20 workmen, and the few scattered ranchers would have no chance.

Taking six men, John Sutter rode swiftly from the fort. It was a grim, silent ride that brought them to the Indian hideout before dawn the following morning. Carefully Sutter stationed his men. At a given signal they thundered into the hideout. Guns crashed. Six Indians died.

"None of my men had been killed or wounded," Sutter recalled later. "I told them [the Indians] that everything would be forgotten if they would come back to the village [fort] and attend to their work as before."

This raid ended much of the "troublesomeness" of the Indians and helped Sutter to "get along very nicely with them."

At first Sutter paid his Indian workers with beads and trinkets or pieces of clothing. Later he had his blacksmiths make round pieces of tin, stamped with a star. One was given to each Indian at the end of a working day. These "coins" could be traded back to Sutter for clothing, blankets, or food.

When white men obtained these "coins," either by fair means or otherwise, John Sutter refused to trade goods for them. Only the Indians who had worked for it could spend the tin "money" for Sutter's goods.

Sutter fed his workers, but not their families. Each morning the workers assembled at the sound of bells and drums. During the harvest season there might be as many as 500 laborers. Their food was a boiled grain cooked in a huge kettle and offered to them in a trough. They were also given daily rations of meat and bread. As soon as they had eaten, the workers marched off in almost military order to the fields.

Having given orders for the day's work, John Sutter would watch them leave, then turn and walk to a small house near the kitchen. Here he and his assistants ate. Roast beef was the main food, morning, noon, or night.

A vegetable garden was maintained just outside the fort. But drought and poor gardening methods made it an uncertain source of food. When Sutter didn't have coffee beans, he made a coffee-like drink with acorns. Sutter said, it "was difficult to tell acorn coffee from the real beverage." Butter, bread, and eggs were also served.

To grind flour for the bread, Sutter had what he called a mule mill, a mill run by mule power. Four mules walked round and round in a circle turning huge mill wheels made of stone. Every four hours fresh mules were hitched to the stones. Sutter often had his mill and his bakery working day and night to furnish the needed bread. Some of Sutter's workmen called the bread "adobe bread." They claimed it was as hard as the adobe bricks he used in the walls of his fort.

There were other Indians who lived in the Sacramento Valley, but who did not work at Sutter's Fort. They lived somewhat differently. They did not try to kill the large animals. They considered bears almost human, while the flesh of dogs was thought to be poisonous. Coyotes and eagles were worshiped and so were not killed or eaten. These Indians ate rabbits, squirrels, and some fish, but their main foods were acorns, herbs, and grass seeds.

Acorns were plentiful, easily gathered, easily stored, and nutritious. Their only drawback was their tannic acid. It was too strong for the human stomach and had to be removed. First the acorns were pounded into a powder, which was spread out over sand. Then boiling water was poured over it. The boiling water dissolved the acid and made the nut flour edible. The flour was then mixed with berries, meat, or even grasshoppers for a nutritious meal.

An Indian mother pounds acorns in a woven container outside her grass mat lodge.

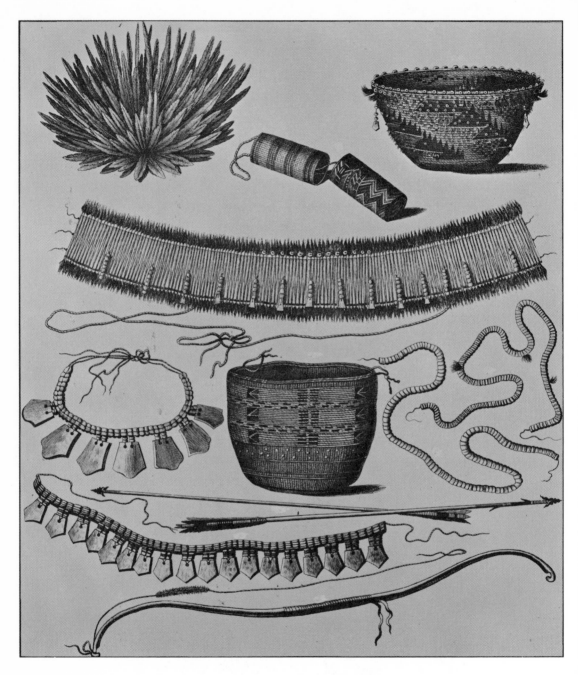

Beautifully woven baskets, used both for cooking and storage, and shell ornaments were made by the California Indians. Shells were used as money, too.

The California Indians wove straw baskets, which they used for hats, for storage, and even for cooking. Since a basket cannot be placed on a fire, basket cooking was done by "stone boiling." The Indians heated stones and then dropped them into the "waterproofed" baskets that were filled with the food they wanted to cook.

Captain Sutter ruled over the 10,000 Indians in the Sacramento Valley and along the Sierra Nevada foothills. He employed them, protected them from neighboring tribes, and even stepped in to settle family disputes.

On one occasion, for instance, a band of Consumnes Indians asked Sutter's permission to trade with the Indians along the American River. Sutter granted the permission. Instead of trading, however, the Consumnes killed a number of the warriors and ran off with their women and children. The women they planned to keep, but the children they intended to sell as slaves.

Sutter soon heard of the treachery from an old man who had escaped. He set out with 20 white men and a large party of Indians. They caught up with the outlaw band about 30 miles below Sutter's Fort. After only a short fight the outlaw Indians were captured. Fourteen of them confessed to killing the American River Indians.

Another time, the young men from a nearby Indian village complained to Sutter that they could not find wives.

Sutter asked, "And why not?"

"Because the chiefs have them all."

At this Sutter frowned. "You mean the chiefs have more than one wife?"

"Yes! They have many, many wives."

The Swiss ruler of the Sacramento may have thought of his own wife and children at home in Europe when he heard this. Years had passed since he had seen them. It had been a long time since he had heard from them or about them.

"Humm. We will take care of that," he declared.

With the young men he rode back to the village. Taking a definite, no-foolishness attitude, he had the women stand in one line and the men in another. To the women he said, "Pick you a husband, the one you want most." To the chiefs he announced, "From now on you may have one wife, maybe two, but no more than that."

John Sutter enjoyed being head of everyone and everything at New Helvetia. His own words describe how he felt about being ruler of the Sacramento:

"I kept military discipline at the settlement, but there was at first neither church nor school. No work was done on Sunday, of course, but no attention was given to religious ceremonies by anybody. There was no clergy, and at burials and marriages I officiated myself. I was everything—patriarch, priest, father, and judge."

Before long, the empire Sutter ruled would become even larger.

4. Vaqueros

The Russians, too, had a fort in California. Called Fort Ross, it was located on the coast near the Russian settlement of Bodega at Bodega Bay.

Fort Ross had been built by a group of Russians 27 years before John Sutter arrived in California. They had reached California by way of the Bering Strait and Alaska. The group was part of the Russian-American Fur Company, owned and operated by the Russian government.

The Russians had come to California for two reasons. First they had come for furs—especially seal and sea otter furs. In this they were all too successful. In 1812, the year they arrived, they had taken more than 40,000 of the animals. But by 1839, the year Sutter arrived, the take had dropped to fewer than 400, and the large herds were becoming almost extinct.

The Russians had also come to raise grain, vegetables, cattle, and sheep for the Russian colony at Sitka, Alaska. In this they were not very successful. There was hardly enough suitable land for their grain. Gophers and rabbits destroyed their vegetables and fruit trees.

By 1841 Fort Ross had become such a disappointment that the Russians were ready to leave. Captain John Sutter bought them out. He bought the buildings at both Fort Ross and Bodega, the farms, cattle, implements, and a schooner. The price was thirty thousand dollars, with a down payment of two thousand dollars. The rest Sutter was to pay mainly in wheat.

As soon as the deal had been completed, Sutter arranged to have all his new possessions moved to his own fort on the Sacramento.

He sent vaqueros for the livestock, which included 1,700 head of cattle, 940 horses and mules, and 900 sheep. The vaqueros were expert Mexican and Indian horsemen who had spent most of their lives handling cattle. Even they had a hard time driving the animals from Bodega and Fort Ross to Sutter's Fort, 125 miles over rough, sometimes timbered, roadless country. They managed the job well until they reached the Sacramento River.

There the cattle balked, refusing to cross the river.

The vaqueros shouted and yelled and lashed at the cattle with their lassos. The cattle in the rear pushed against those in the lead, forcing them into the rushing river.

Bellowing with fright, the cattle in front tried to turn. But the stock in back crowded against them, shoving them deeper into the water. At last the leaders twisted around and started swimming for the opposite shore. Others followed. The vaqueros, still yelling and flinging their ropes, reached the river and rode into it.

When the cattle reached the opposite shore, almost 100 were missing. They had been swept down the river and drowned. But the vaqueros

found their carcasses, or dead bodies, and skinned them. The cattle were worth almost as much dead as alive.

John Sutter accepted his loss with a simple statement, "Fortunately we were able to save most of the hides, at that time the real bank-notes of California."

The people at Sutter's Fort could hear the cattle long before they arrived. The sound of their bellowing mingled with the clashing of their horns and the shouts of the vaqueros.

When they reached the fort, the vaqueros stopped driving and let the cattle spread out across the dry autumn grass. A horseman left the herd and rode to the top of the hill where Sutter stood waiting.

Sutter greeted him and asked, "Now that we've got them here, José, how will we keep them from running right back to Bodega Bay?"

A huge smile flashed across José's dark face. His white teeth sparkled in the sunshine. "You will see, senor! You will see."

For three days the cattle were left alone. At first they grazed close to Sutter's Fort. But gradually the more venturesome began moving farther and farther away.

On the third day the vaqueros held a round-up. They called it a *rodeo*. Yelling and scream-ing at the top of their voices, they chased the cattle back to an open area near the fort where they could be bunched together. The slow ones and those that tried to hide in the bush were lashed with the lassos. The men yelled at them while the horses almost ran over them.

"Next time they will come much faster," José explained to Sutter. John Sutter and all the men from the fort were outside watching the roundup. "Some of them will not want to stay. When they try to run away, we will have more fun." Sweat ran down José's face.

Suddenly a huge bull whirled about and raced away from the herd. In an instant a horse and rider shot after it. The vaquero was yelling with glee and spurring his mount.

In only a moment the horse was beside the bull. With one quick movement the vaquero reached down and grabbed the bull's tail. Another yell and the horse seemed to shoot ahead. The rider gave a twist and a turn of the tail, and the bull flipped end over end across the hard ground.

By the time the rider had stopped, the bull was again on its feet. One more yell from the vaquero, and the unhurt bull raced back to the herd as fast as it could go.

"He will likely try it one more time, senor," José grinned. "He will think he can fool us by holding his tail down under his belly. But we will find it, and whoossh! Over he goes again." José threw up his hands and rolled them to show the bull tumbling over and over. "Every day or so now, we will drive them here like this. After a while all we need to do is yell, and they will come running. It is a good way to watch the cattle, no?"

John Sutter had to grin back at the happy vaquero. "Yes, it is a good way, José."

The vaqueros' work also included the butchering. Two of them would go out and select the fattest and best animal they could find. They would drive it close to the fort. One of them would rope it by the horns while the other roped it by the hind legs. After it had been killed, they would stretch it out and skin it there on the ground. All the meat was used and the fats were saved for cooking.

One vaquero has already roped the steer's legs, and another swings his lasso to catch his horns in this painting of the "California mode of catching cattle."

Cattle hides were hung on racks to dry at a *matanza*.

During the *matanza*, or regular butchering season, 50 or even 100 steers would be killed at one time. The slaughter usually occurred during the winter or spring and kept the vaqueros really busy.

The animals were killed, skinned, and the skins stretched out to dry in the usual way. Now all the fat was boiled in large kettles. As it cooled it was ladled into a smaller container and a stick placed in the center of it. When the tallow had completely hardened, the stick served as a handle. A fat steer might produce 100 pounds of tallow.

Only the choice pieces of beef were kept

now. The rest was left for the wild wolves and bears that came down from the hills in the night to gorge themselves. Then the vaqueros went out to rope and kill the huge grizzly bears.

Sometimes the riders would rope and kill elk and deer in another wild and dangerous sport. The hides and tallow from these animals were sold with the tallow and hides from the cattle. They often were traded to the skippers of Yankee clipper ships from New England. In the United States the tallow was made into candles and soap; the hides were tanned and the leather made into shoes.

Then the fat was boiled to obtain tallow for candles.

Vaqueros, swinging their lassos, plunge into a herd
of wild horses in this painting by Arthur Nahl.

Sometimes the vaqueros killed wild horses
when they became too numerous. Thousands
of wild horses roamed over the hills and
through the valleys. During times of drought
they invaded the ranches, devouring the sparse
grass and drinking the water from the drying
waterholes.

A herd of wild horses lived in the thickets
back of the Russian River where the Russians
had been. When John Bidwell, Sutter's clerk
in charge of Bodega and Fort Ross, tried to
capture them or kill them, they got away.

Finally Bidwell made a contract with a vaquero named Manuel Saez to catch them. Manuel was master with the lasso. But Manuel and his men could not capture the herd.

"For ten days they labored with utmost effort," Bidwell reported. "In that time they lassoed nine grizzly bears, one black bear, many elk, antelope and deer—but they only caught five of the wild horses."

Wild grizzly bears were common in California and easier to lasso than the wild horses of the Russian River. John Bidwell told of another occasion when he and some vaqueros came upon a grizzly bear mother and her two cubs.

Yelling and screaming, Bidwell and the vaqueros charged. They swung their lassos like whips and soon had the mother bear going one way and the cubs another.

Two lassos dropped down over the cubs and held them firm. The excitement was suddenly over. The men sat on their panting horses and grinned at each other and then at the silent cubs. "Now that we have them," one of the vaqueros asked, "what will we do with them?"

"Why, take them back to the rancho, of course," the other vaquero answered. "They will make wonderful pets."

The men again looked at each other, grinning now like mischievous boys. "And who," the first vaquero asked doubtfully, "will take them back to the rancho?"

"Why, you, of course. Who else could be trusted with such an important job?"

In spite of the vaquero's protests, the cubs' paws were tied together, and the cubs were fastened one on each side of his saddle. He mounted. Everything was very quiet now. Even the horses had stopped chomping the dried grass. The vaquero looked at the others and licked his dry lips.

Hunting grizzly bears was sometimes sport, but often a necessity in California's forests.

Before he could speak, one of them whispered, "If you should meet the mama, you must not stop to gossip."

All the men laughed loudly. Their guffaws frightened the cubs, and they cried out for help. A great roar sounded from the nearby brush. Branches snapped and cracked as the mother grizzly crashed through the heavy undergrowth and shot toward the startled vaqueros.

Horses leaped away in every direction. The one with the cubs jumped into the air, twisting, turning, and tossing off the vaquero. At the same time, the saddle to which the cubs were tied slid under the horse's belly, spilling the cubs to the ground while the frightened horse fled in panic.

When the bear family got together again, the mother promptly led them back into the hills. Somewhere she was sure to find a safer place to raise a pair of grizzly cubs.

John Bidwell later told the end of the story: "Nothing but the speed of our horses saved us from that enraged mother bear. Fortunately for the unseated vaquero there was a tree close at hand; up he climbed and it was too small for her to follow."

5. Sutter's Army

More than cattle, horses, and sheep came to New Helvetia from Fort Ross. Lumber and all the farming implements which had belonged to the Russians were shipped to Sutter's Fort aboard the former Russian schooner *Constantine*, which Sutter renamed the *Sacramento*. Sutter's purchases included materials for a gristmill for grinding grain and a tanning shop.

In addition, he received a large supply of ammunition, several cannons, and a good many flintlock muskets. The muskets were said to have been those left by Napoleon's troops during their retreat from Moscow in 1812.

Of the ammunition John Sutter bragged, "At times I had more ammunition stored up than the whole California government possessed."

Moving everything from Bodega and Fort Ross to Sutter's Fort took two years. By this time Sutter's own fort was taking form. It was now enclosed by adobe walls two and a half feet thick. At two corners Sutter built bastions, towers extending outside the fort walls, with cannons and portholes. From the portholes, a defender could look down upon an approaching enemy and use the cannon to stop him, before he even reached the walls. Beneath the bastions were prisons.

Sutter's "army" was also taking shape. He had a "home guard" of young Indian braves. "The Indian boys," Sutter wrote, "were obliged to appear every Sunday morning for drill, well washed and neatly clad. Their uniforms consisted of blue . . . pantaloons, white . . . shirts, and red handkerchiefs tied around their heads."

The young Indians were proud of their uniforms and seemed to enjoy the military discipline and the sharp, barking commands of their Swiss and German "officers."

Sutter's personal bodyguards were what he
called "grown-up soldiers." They had regular
uniforms of blue and green, which had been
purchased along with the other materials at
Fort Ross. The bodyguards, who were also
Indians, occupied quarters near Sutter's own
bedroom so as to be ready to act in any
emergency.

"I had a half-hour glass installed," Sutter said, "and during the night the guards struck the bell every time the sand ran out, and cried, 'All is well'; summer and winter at daybreak, the bell was rung for all hands to get up and go to work."

John Sutter's army was indeed a strange mixture. Swiss and German officers commanded Indian soldiers in a land belonging to Mexico! The uniforms were from Russia while the muskets they carried were castoffs from defeated French troops.

Sutter's Indian servants had to be dressed correctly too. In 1843 Sutter wrote a letter to the owner of a trading post in Yerba Buena, as San Francisco was called then. In the letter he asked for a supply of brown cloth to make clothes for his servants "who are in rags and naked, and when strangers come it looks very bad."

No one knows whether Sutter ever got the cloth he needed to dress his staff properly. We do know though that, as time went on, more and more of these "strangers" arrived at Sutter's Fort to see for themselves the strange empire which the Swiss Captain had built in the Sacramento Valley.

6. Activities at the Fort

In March, 1844 two men rode into Sutter's Fort, so weak from hunger and exhaustion they could hardly stay in their saddles. One was Kit Carson, trapper, guide, and scout. The other was John C. Frémont, explorer and map maker.

Frémont had charge of an official expedition for the United States Topographical Corps. His job was to explore and map much of the western territory belonging to the United States. His stricken party was still camped back on the Sierra Nevada slopes in need of help.

Sutter immediately provided food for Carson and Frémont. Then he sent men and ten mules loaded with supplies back to their companions. Frémont remained the night with Sutter, but Kit Carson accompanied the supplies back into the mountains.

The whole expedition was in bad shape. Half their horses and mules had been lost or eaten. Clothing and bedding were in tatters. Saddles and bridles were worn out.

John Frémont camped near the fort for three weeks while Sutter re-outfitted the expedition. It was a busy and exciting three weeks. Vaqueros were sent out to round up horses, mules, and cattle. Fires glowed brightly all day long in the blacksmith's forge, and the clanging of hammers was a constant sound as the smiths put new shoes on Frémont's surviving horses. The mule mill worked day and night grinding flour. In the saddle shop, the saddlemakers built new pack and riding saddles.

In all John Sutter sold Frémont thirty horses, eighty mules, several fat cattle, clothing, provisions, and saddles. He sold everything at cost and accepted as payment government credit orders. The Topographical Bureau in

Washington, D. C. would eventually give Sutter money in exchange for these orders, but Sutter soon needed the cash. He had to sell his government credit orders to others at a twenty per cent discount. By doing this he lost one dollar out of every five on all the goods he sold Frémont.

This transaction illustrates why Captain John Sutter was always in serious financial trouble. He was not a good businessman. He was overly generous to anyone in need; he sold goods on credit when he could not wait for payment; and he bought more on credit than he could afford.

Kit Carson (standing) and John C. Fremont, whom he guided to California.

In seeking to pay off his debts, Sutter tried many different ways of making money in the Sacramento Valley. Instead of sending all his hides to be tanned into leather in the United States, he started his own tannery. Since the tanning of hides makes a very unpleasant smell, the tannery was far from the fort.

To start the tanning the workmen placed dried or salted hides in large vats, or tubs, filled with water and lime. After soaking the hides, the men spread them out on the ground. On hands and knees, the tanners now crawled over the hides with scrapers in their hands. It was hard work to remove all the hair. Once it was done, the workers again washed the hides, next placing them in vats of weak tannic acid. After a few days, the workmen moved them from the first vat to vat number two, which contained a stronger solution of tannic acid, and finally on to vat number three containing a still stronger solution.

To make the tannic solution the other workmen, known as peelers, went out into the hills and scraped the bark from tanbark oak trees. They then pounded the bark into a powder which was added to water, making a solution known as tan liquor.

Some of the leather was used by Sutter's shoemakers and saddlemakers. The rest was sold to ranchers and businessmen.

John Sutter made candles from some of his tallow. The small candle room was hot and smelly. In one corner a fireplace heated a large kettle of tallow. Sweating workmen dipped the tallow from the kettle and poured it into wooden tubs that looked much like the bottom halves of wooden barrels. Above each tub there was a wooden frame from which 20 or more strings dangled down. The workmen dipped the strings into the hot tallow, held them for only a moment, then lifted them again. Not all the hot tallow dripped back into the tub. Some cooled, encasing each string within a thin sheaf of tallow. Again they were dipped down into the warm, fluid mixture and again lifted out. This same action went on time after time until the slow buildup of tallow grew into a candle the right size and shape. Candles made this way were usually rough and uneven, but they gave just as good light as those made in a mold.

Molds were made of metal and resembled several empty pipes joined together. These "pipes" tapered down and at the end had only

a tiny hole. String was threaded through the center of each mold, and all of them were filled with tallow. When cooled, the molds were dipped into hot water, and the candles could easily be pulled out. These candles were uniform in shape and size. Their sides were smooth, and they were in demand by the people of California.

Sutter also did fur trading on a small scale. He sent Indians to hunt and trap throughout the Sacramento Valley. Records show that in 1842 Sutter sent 140 beaver skins and 30 otter skins to a creditor named Don Antonio. He was credited with $2.50 per pound for the beaver furs and $2.50 each for the otter skins.

Sutter conducted a fishing enterprise on a larger scale. During the years of 1840 and 1841 several schooner loads of salmon, which had been caught by Sutter's Indians, were shipped to San Francisco. There they were fresh-salted or smoked and then sold to local residents and incoming ships.

Farming, ranching, and related efforts were the main money-making activities of Sutter's vast empire. In one room of the fort blankets were woven of the wool taken from Sutter's sheep. Many Indian women at New Helvetia had learned to weave at the early Spanish missions. They had become expert weavers. The blankets they produced were in great demand.

Wheat was the principal farm product. But it was an uncertain crop. Sutter had agreed to pay the Russians mostly in wheat, but he was never able to raise enough of it to meet his obligation. In 1840 he had little seed, poor plows, and inexperienced workers. In the two following years, drought cut his yield so low he hardly replaced his seed.

There were, however, some good years. Three or four hundred Indians would then move into the fields for the harvesting. Some had sickles, others had butcher knives, but many had nothing with which to cut the grain. Those with no cutting tools would pull the ripe grain from the ground, roots and all, or they would break off the stalks close to the ground. Soon their hands were sore and bleeding.

After the grain was all cut, it was stacked in the threshing area. Sutter had a wooden threshing floor from Fort Ross, which was superior to the dry ground. A fence was built around the stacked grain. Three or four hundred wild horses were driven into the threshing area. The Indians would wave their arms and whoop and yell to make the horses race around and around. After a time the Indians would suddenly dash in front of the racing horses, whooping and yelling even louder. The frightened horses would now reverse their direction, driving their feet to the very bottom of the wheat. In this way as much as 2000 bushels of wheat could be threshed in a single hour.

After the threshing came the winnowing, which was done only when the wind was blowing. Shovelfuls of the grain, straw, and chaff (seed coverings) were thrown high into the air. While the heavier grain fell almost straight down, the lighter straw and chaff were blown away for some distance. Winnowing sometimes took a long time, but it was the only way to make the grain ready for milling into flour.

7. A Young Settler Tells About Sutter's Fort

Slowly the white population at Sutter's Fort grew. Sailors slipped off their ships, hid in the woods until their ships sailed, then came into the fort and asked for employment. John Frémont had discharged three of his men on his first visit. John Sutter employed them, one as a blacksmith.

In the fall of 1845 a party in eight wagons arrived at the fort on the Sacramento River. They had traveled well, and their wagons, animals, and the people themselves were in good condition. One of them was Benjamin Franklin Bonney, a boy of eight.

Later, in a booklet entitled *Across the Plains by Prairie Schooner*, Bonney recalled:

"When we arrived at the fort, Captain Sutter made us heartily welcome . . . . He furnished us quarters in the fort and also gave us plenty of fresh beef, potatoes, onions, coffee, and sugar . . . . He gave work to all the men who cared to work. Some of the men helped break the wild Spanish cattle to plow."

California's early plowing methods were far from efficient. Four oxen were used to pull a crude plow. Instead of yokes, the animals had poles tied to their horns. Rawhide strips tied the poles to the plow. Three men were needed to drive them. One led them while the other two walked, one on each side, to goad them with long sharp sticks.

Benjamin Bonney's father made regular ox yokes to fit on the animals' shoulders. Other men worked with the wild cattle. A yoke of tame oxen was placed in front, a yoke of wild cattle in the middle, and finally, another yoke of tame oxen in back. When the driver

cracked his whip and yelled, the tame oxen started out. Other men prodded the wild cattle while keeping out of the way of the slashing horns. At first it was a contest of strength, but with two oxen pulling in front and another two pushing in back, the wild cattle were literally dragged across the field. After a while they found it was easier and safer to walk. Before long they started to follow the commands themselves.

Benjamin Bonney was a normal eight-year-old. He was in and out of everything, interested in everything that happened, and fascinated by everything he saw. He especially liked hitching rides in the small, two-wheeled Mexican carts called *carretas*.

These carts were hard riding and noisy. Each wheel was made from solid oak almost a foot thick. A hole was cut in the center of the wheel for the axle, which was made from a tree limb. The body of the cart rested on the axle. Small, round limbs were used to build a framework for the sides of the carretas.

The carts, pulled by oxen, had many uses. Hides and tallow were hauled to the river where they could be loaded onto schooners.

Grain was hauled to the threshing areas, and the threshed wheat was hauled to the storage bins.

Benjamin never had to worry about missing one of these carts. Their squeaking could often be heard half a mile away. Soap was used to lessen the squeaks and to help the wheels turn easier. The soap was carried in a swinging bucket fastened to the back of the carreta. Sometimes the driver let Bonney spread some of the soap on the smooth, hot axle.

Young Bonney remembered the large cook house where the children liked to watch the cooks prepare the food. Along one wall was a large brick stove which was divided into three parts. Above the firepit on the right, long iron rails held big pots, pans, and kettles up above the fire. These utensils were made of thick metal. They were heavy with a layer of black soot burned onto the outside.

The center section of the stove was used for baking such things as cakes, pies, and puddings. The baking of bread was done in an outside oven. The left section of the stove was used for roasting meat. A framework above the firepit was large enough to hold a

quarter of beef or a whole sheep. An Indian
stood, slowly turning the meat round and round
so it wouldn't burn. The delicious smells from
the kitchen made Benjamin's mouth water.

John Sutter loved good food. He was a
cordial host and never passed up a chance to
celebrate. On Christmas Day, 1845, he entertained six men in his living room in the big
house. Benjamin Bonney didn't go to the
party, but he heard about it and the menu

prepared by Captain Sutter's English cook:

First Course
Beef soup served with frijoles (beans),
red peppers, and garlic

Second Course
Roast beef served with frijoles,
red peppers, and garlic

Third Course
Baked beef pie served with frijoles,
red peppers, and garlic

Fourth Course
Stewed beef served with frijoles,
red peppers, and garlic

Fifth Course
Fried beef served with frijoles,
red peppers, and garlic

Dessert
Christmas Plum Pudding (Mexican style),
made from beef tallow, sour wild grapes,
chili, and black pepper

The cook didn't have the regular spices for making a traditional English Plum Pudding, so he used the spices he had—chili and black pepper.

When one guest bit into the fiery mixture he demanded, "Cook! What is this?"

"Why, sir," the cook replied with a slight smile, "it's Christmas Plum Pudding, Mexican style."

That winter Sutter's Fort was crowded. John Sutter recollected:

> "All the buildings and houses of my settlement were filled . . . with wet, hungry, poor immigrants—men, women, and children. Sometimes the houses were so full of people that I could hardly find a place to sleep."

Sickness came; many of the Indians and some of the white people died. Benjamin Bonney's older brother and his sister Ann both died that winter and were buried at Sutter's Fort. "In those days it was called mountain fever," Benjamin Bonney explained. "Now it is called typhoid fever."

Spring, 1846 brought warm sunshine, fresh air—and the Mexican army. Friendly relations between Mexico and the United States had been broken off. Californians were seeking ways of getting the Americans to leave.

For some time the Californians had been afraid of John Sutter and the Americans who lived at his fort. They did not like Sutter issuing passports to the Americans, feeding them, and protecting them. These passports were papers which permitted their owners to remain and travel in California. Now the Californians decreed that passports were not enough. The Americans would have to become Mexican citizens or leave.

"Stay," John Sutter urged his friends. "I will give you land and help you get started." But the Bonneys and many others decided to go on to Oregon.

"Oh, how can we?" Mrs. Bonney asked,

tears wetting her eyes. "There are no wagon roads, and Ellen Francisco cannot ride a horse." Ellen Francisco was Benjamin's baby sister. She had been born at Sutter's Fort and was only a few months old.

An old Scotsman finally solved this problem. He made pack saddles with high arms. Around a framework he wove baskets of rawhide. Two children could be placed in each pack so there would be the least possible danger.

Sutter helped many Americans settle in California. His blacksmith, Peter Lassen, became the owner of this prosperous ranch.

Young Benjamin later wrote in his book:

"I will never forget the exciting forenoon we spent when we started from the fort. Many of the horses were not saddle broken and when the children were put in these high pack saddles the horses would run and buck. At first many of the children set up a terrible clamor, but when they found they were not spilled out, they greatly enjoyed the excitement. Their mothers were frantic."

Sutter gave each family a fat beef animal and sent ten Mexican vaqueros to drive the loose stock and teach the Americans how to load a pack saddle.

8. Gold!

In 1846 the United States and Mexico were at war. Then came the Bear Flag Revolt which proclaimed that California was free from Mexico. Sutter took little part in this.

On the morning of June 14, 1846, a group of Americans from the Sacramento Valley arrived at the town of Sonoma. Here they arrested General Vallejo and three other leaders. They hoisted a flag on which had been drawn a grizzly bear. And they declared California an independent republic.

John C. Frémont was not at Sonoma, but his camp in the Sacramento Valley had been the meeting place for the rebels. And John Frémont was in full sympathy with the movement. Soon he resigned from the United States Army and became its leader.

One of his first acts was to move everything to Sutter's Fort. Captain John Sutter threw open his gates and welcomed them. In this way he joined the rebellion.

When Frémont took complete charge, Sutter was angry. He resented being little more than a servant in his own fort. He also disliked being in charge of the prisoners from Sonoma.

"When the prisoners arrived at the Fort," he wrote at a later date, "I placed my best rooms at their disposal and treated them with every consideration . . . The gentlemen took their meals with me and walked with me in the evening."

Frémont disapproved of this special consideration for prisoners. "Don't you know how to treat prisoners of war?" he asked Sutter.

"Indeed I do," Sutter replied and immediately refused to remain in charge of the prisoners.

"The prisoners were then placed in the

charge of Bidwell, who allowed them just as much liberty as they enjoyed when they were in my care," Sutter wrote.

Bidwell taught one of the prisoners English and received lessons in Spanish in return.

The Bear Flag Revolt lasted only a short time. Then the forces of the United States moved into California and declared it a part of that country. The American flag was raised at Monterey and Yerba Buena. At Sonoma the Bear Flag, which had flown only three weeks, was lowered and the Stars and Stripes raised in its place.

An American flag was sent to Sutter's Fort.

The American flag waved triumphantly over Sutter's Fort when American forces marched into California.

"A long time before daybreak I had the whole Fort alarmed," Sutter later explained, "and my guns ready. When the Star Spangled Banner slowly rose on the flag staff, the cannon began to fire and continued until nearly all the windows were broken."

A few days later the prisoners were all released.

When Frémont left Sutter's Fort to continue fighting to the south, he took with him, according to John Sutter, all his workmen and all his best Indians. Once again John Sutter had little chance of a bountiful harvest.

The United States Army won this battle at La Mesa between Mexican lancers and the forces of General Kearney.

When the Mexican War was over, California, Utah, Nevada, and New Mexico were added to the United States.

New Helvetia continued to grow. More workers were hired. Sutter put more land under cultivation. Animals multiplied, and the herds became larger.

"I had several hundred workers in the harvest fields," Sutter wrote of the year 1847. "To feed them I had to kill four and sometimes five oxen daily."

Sutter estimated his livestock then at 12,000 head of cattle, 2,000 horses and mules, 10,000 to 15,000 sheep and 1,000 hogs. He could raise 40,000 bushels of wheat per season. Since he could not grind this much wheat into flour, he was having a new gristmill built at Natoma. Since lumber was needed for the flour mill, a sawmill was started further up the American River at a place named Coloma.

James W. Marshall was in charge of building this sawmill. On the morning of January 28, 1848, Marshall arrived at Sutter's Fort. Rain was streaming down, and Marshall was wet to the skin. He rode in through the main gate and swung down into the mud. John Sutter appeared in one of the doorways, and Marshall sloshed through the mud to meet him.

"Is there somewhere we can talk in private?" Marshall asked.

Sutter nodded and led him into a small room. Marshall dropped several yellow nuggets on top of a small, rough-boarded table. He said, "They came from the mill site at Coloma."

The nuggets were weighed and tested, and John Sutter announced, "They're gold all right. Almost pure gold!"

With the discovery of gold, John Sutter

Sutter's Mill at Coloma where gold in California was first discovered.

faced two immediate problems. Since the mill site was outside his grant from Governor Alvarado, Sutter tried to get a deed to the land before others learned of the discovery. He was unsuccessful. He also tried to keep word of the gold discovery from the public. Again he was unsuccessful.

This discovery of gold started the great California Gold Rush of 1849. Thousands of people migrated to California. Doctors, lawyers, merchants, farmers, butchers, and bakers all streamed to the Sacramento Valley. They came afoot, on horseback, by covered wagon,

These miners sluicing gold were typical of those who
poured onto Sutter's property to seek their fortune.

and by clipper ship, believing that California was a land of gold, and that everyone would become rich.

What really happened was that a few did get rich, many died of sickness and starvation, and some turned to robbery and murder.

Sutter's own men went looking for gold. His crops were left untended and destroyed. His animals were stolen. Many of his buildings, apart from the fort, were ripped down. The lumber was used for miners' shacks and equipment.

Sutter sold food and other articles needed by the miners at high prices. But the money this brought in was not enough to offset Sutter's heavy losses. Sutter began to drink heavily, and that hastened his downfall.

During this period Sutter's oldest son arrived at the fort. Father and son had a happy reunion, but the happiness was brief. Sutter's money troubles intruded upon it. John Sutter had never finished paying the Russian-American Fur Company for the property he purchased at Bodega and Fort Ross. Now the company was demanding payment. Other creditors were also demanding payment of money he owed them.

By 1849, the little town of Sacramento had become a busy river port.

In order to save himself from the complete financial ruin that would result from the payment of his debts, John Sutter transferred all his property to his son, John Sutter, Jr.

Young Sutter was only 21 years old and inexperienced in the American business world. He was serious and hard-working. He did everything he could to aid and protect his father. His largest venture was the sale of business lots along the Sacramento River.

These were part of the New Helvetia grant. Money from the sales helped young John Sutter to pay many of his father's debts. The sale of these business lots represented the actual beginning of the city of Sacramento.

John Sutter finally had to sell his fort. He then moved further north to his farm on the Feather River. There at last he was reunited with his wife and the rest of his children.

Sutter's fortune continued to vanish. More of his cattle, horses, mules, and sheep were stolen and slaughtered.

Then the squatters came. A squatter was a man who settled on a piece of land and claimed it for his own. The squatters refused to recognize land grants issued by the Mexican government. John Sutter and many early California citizens suffered great losses from the claims of the squatters.

For years Sutter's Fort deteriorated. The walls crumbled and fell down until only the big house remained. Then in 1888 a movement was started to save the old historical site. Twenty thousand dollars were raised, and in 1891 reconstruction was started.

Today the reconstructed Sutter's Fort stands just off U.S. Highway 99 near the heart of

Sacramento. Here visitors can see how the people worked and lived in the 1840's. The clothes they wore, the tools they used, the chairs they sat on, and the tables they ate from are all preserved. Oak and sycamore trees rise above the fort. At one side is a huge, gnarled cottonwood tree. The gardener says it was there as a small tree when John Sutter lived in the fort and ruled the Sacramento Valley—the one living thing to see the whole story.

Glossary

adobe: brick made of clay dried in the sun

amigo: a Spanish word meaning friend

bastion: a tower extending beyond the main wall of a fort

carreta: a small, two-wheeled Mexican cart

chaff: seed coverings of wheat or other grain

cooper: a barrel maker

frijoles: Spanish word for beans

gristmill: a mill for grinding grain

Helvetia: Latin word for Switzerland

Kanaka: native of the Hawaiian Islands

matanza: a Spanish word meaning the butchering season

nugget: a lump or a rough piece, especially of gold ore

rawhide: cattle hide that is not yet made into leather

rodeo: the Spanish word for a roundup of cattle

sickle: a tool with a curved blade and a short handle

squatter: a person who settles on a piece of land and claims it as his own without a right or title to it

stock: livestock, such as cattle, horses, etc.

tallow: the hard fat of cows, melted for use in candles and soap

tannery: a place where animal hides are made into leather

tannic acid: an acid obtained from oak bark, used in tanning leather

thresh: to separate the seed or grain from wheat by beating

vaquero: Spanish word for cowboy

winnow: to blow away the chaff from grain

Index

A

Across the Plains by Prairie Schooner, 71
Adobe bricks, 25–26
Adz, 26
Alaska, 42–43
Alvarado, Governor Juan Bautista, 17, 28, 87
American River, 13, 39–40, 86
Amigos, 20

B

Bartleson, John, 13
Bears, 5 (pic), 36, 51, 53–55, 54 (pic)
Bering Strait, 42
Bidwell, John, 7–9, 11, 13–16, 52–53, 55, 83
Bodega, 42–45, 57, 89
Bodega Bay, 46
Bonney, Benjamin, 70–71, 73–75, 77, 79–80

C

California, 8, 13, 16–17, 20, 23–24, 42–43, 46, 53, 71, 78, 81, 83, 85, 87, 89, 91
Carretas, 25 (pic), 73–74
Carson, Kit, 60–61, 62 (pic)
Cattle raising, 18, 23–24, 33, 42 (pic), 43–50, 48 (pic), 49 (pic), 56, 71–72, 85
Coloma, 86

Consumnes, 39
Constantine, 56

E

Echoes of the Past, 13–15

F

Fort Ross, 42–44, 56–68, 89
Fremont, John C., 60–62, 62 (pic), 70, 82, 84
Furs, 43, 66, 89

G

Gold, Discovery of, 86–87, 87 (pic), 88 (pic), 89

H

Helvetia, 22
Horses, Wild, 18, 52–53, 52 (pic), 80
Hunting, 5 (pic), 18, 36, 51–55, 52 (pic), 54 (pic), 80

I

Indians, 9, 14, 17–18, 19 (pic), 20, 22, 24–26, 28, 30–36, 30 (pic), 37 (pic), 38 (pic), 39–40, 44, 57–59, 66–68, 84
Isabella, 22

K

Kanakas, 23–24

L

Lassen, Peter, 11
Lassen's Ranch, 78–79 (pic)

M

Matanza, 50 (pic), 51
Marshall, John, 86
Mexican War, 77, 81–85, 81 (pic), 84–85 (pic)
Mexico, 13, 16, 77, 81
Missouri, 13
Monterey, 17, 28 (pic), 83

N

Nevada, 13
New Helvetia, 22, 23, 28–29, 33, 41, 56, 66, 85, 91
Nicholas, 22

R

Rodeo, 47 (pic), 49 (pic)
Russian River, 52–53
Russians, 42–43

S

Sacramento, 23, 41, 90 (pic), 91
Sacramento, 56
Sacramento Valley, 16, 17, 28, 36, 39–40, 59, 63, 66, 81–82, 92
San Francisco, 22, 59, 66, *see also* Yerba Buena
Sierra Nevada, 13, 14, 39, 69
Sitka, Alaska, 43
Sonoma, 81–83
Spanish missions, 20
Squatters, 91
Sutter, John Augustus, 9 (pic), 11, 13, 14–20, 22–26, 28–

36, 39–43, 46–47,
49, 52, 56–59, 61–
64, 66–67, 70–71,
75–78, 80–87, 89,
92
Sutter, John, Jr., 89–
91
Sutter's Army, 57–
59
Sutter's Fort, 2 (pic),
29 (pic), 83 (pic)
building of, 24–26,
29
deterioration of, 89–
91
development of, 56–
59, 70, 71, 85
location of, 13, 22–
23
restoration of, 91–92

Sutter's Fort, Activi-
ties at,
barrelmaking, 11
brickmaking, 25
blacksmith shop, 11
candlemaking, 50
(pic), 64
cattle raising, 18,
23–24, 33, 42
(pic), 43–50, 48
(pic), 49 (pic),
56, 71–72, 85
farming, 25 (pic),
30 (pic), 66–69
gristmill, 56
tanning, 50 (pics),
56, 63
weaving, 38 (pic),
67
Sutter's Mill, 86–87,
87 (pic)

T

Travelers, 13, 14–15,
15 (pic), 59, 70–
71, 70 (pic)

U

United States Army,
82

V

Vallejo, General, 81
Vaqueros, 11, 42, (pic),
44, 47–49, 47 (pic),
49 (pic), 51–55,
52 (pic), 54 (pic),
80

Y

Yerba Buena, 59, 83,
see also San Fran-
cisco

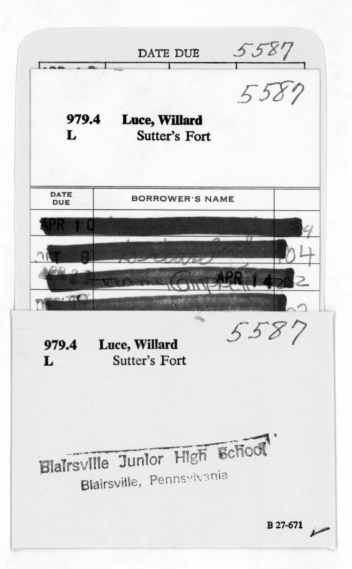

DATE DUE   *5587*

5587

979.4   **Luce, Willard**
L   Sutter's Fort

DATE DUE	BORROWER'S NAME	
APR 1 0		
nT 8		
APR 2 2	APR 1 4 62	

5587

979.4   **Luce, Willard**
L   Sutter's Fort

B 27-671